stitch & s

stitch

&

sparkle

Charlotte Liddle

SPECIAL PHOTOGRAPHY BY
John Heseltine

Coats
Crafts UK

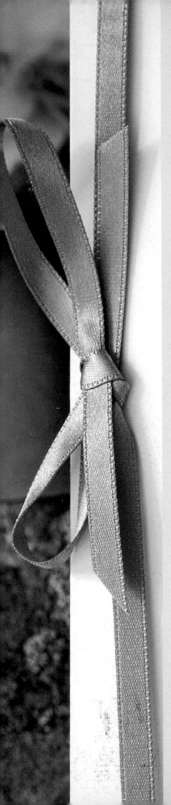

A Coats publication

This edition first published in 2007 by
Coats Crafts UK
Lingfield Point
McMullen Road
Darlington
Co. Durham
DL1 1YQ
UK

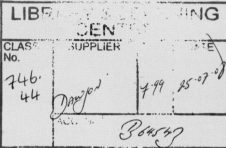
Editor Katie Hardwicke
Design Anne Wilson
Technique photography Charlotte Liddle
Project styling Susan Berry

Publications Manager Dawn Shaefer

British Library Cataloguing in Publication Data
A catalogue record for this book is available from the British Library

ISBN 1-904485-88-X
Reproduced and printed in Malaysia

contents

Introduction

While writing this book I was very conscious of the fact that I wanted to create something that was more inspirational than technical, without being overly concerned with perfection. My aim is that this book will inspire, motivate and encourage a whole range of craftspeople to pick up a needle and thread, and explore the many possibilities of fabric.

So don't worry if you are useless at dress-making or hate the thought of executing stitch-perfect seams, this book is about using innovative embroidery techniques and interesting colour combinations to create modern textiles that certainly do not involve hours of laborious or repetitive stitching.

The fifteen projects have been designed with an emphasis on re-working, recycling and layering, the majority are quick and simple to make and could even be done as craft projects with your children. For those who have a little more experience, I've also added suggestions as to how to take the projects further and move onto more ambitious pieces.

I've used vintage garments and retro curtains along with shop-bought Prym adornments and some beautiful Rowan fabrics to make contemporary accessories from buttons, brooches and bags to quirky little peg dolls and even a pampered pet's coat – so if you have no desire to make something from scratch there are plenty of alternatives: customize, customize, customize!

Once you have mastered the basic appliqué and embellishment techniques, the possibilities of what you can customize are endless. So start collecting like a magpie, save those scraps of old fabrics, buttons, beads and sequins and put them to good use in creating something that is unique and individual for yourself or to give as a gift.

Colour

Choosing colours that go well together can often be challenging and sometimes daunting. All those old tales about pink and red not going together and blue and green never being seen are not really true these days. So be brave and bold, allow your imagination to run wild and you might just be stunned by the results. If you still find it hard, think in terms of "palettes" of colours and go for a hot colour palette (yellows, reds, oranges, bright pinks) or a cool palette (pale blues, mauves, light greens, lemons). All of those who are still little girls at heart may be more attracted to a classic fairy princess palette (shades of pinks and lilacs, with accents of white, baby blue and light green).

Here are three sample "palettes" I put together, just to give you a starting point. You will see that the projects in this book fit, broadly, into one or another of them.

Fairy princess palette

Cool, sophisticated palette

Hot, bright palette

Hand and embroidery stitches

Learning to stitch by hand is like any other skill: practice makes perfect. You will need to be able to use a needle and thread effectively for several of the projects in this book, and some require a little basic hand embroidery, too.

None of the embroidery stitches I have used in this book are hard to master, but if you practise on a scrap of fabric first, your stitches will be neater and more professional looking. You can make your stitches in fine embroidery silks for a delicate effect or in much thicker crewel wool for a more dramatic impact.

You will need an embroidery needle with an eye large enough for the thread or yarn you want to use. The threads you choose can make a considerable difference to the results. Thick, fat yarns will result in a chunky, naïve effect. Embroidery silks will have a much smoother, more delicate appearance. Make sure the yarn you choose is suitable for the ground fabric you are working on, such as wool yarns for felt, and embroidery silks for fine cottons, for example.

Running stitch
This is the simplest embroidery stitch, known as a straight stitch. You simply work from right to left (if right handed) and, working with a thread knotted at one end, you pass the needle and thread in and out of the fabric in a line, taking two of three stitches onto the needle before pulling the needle and thread through the fabric. You can use the stitch to gather up fabric, too.

Chain stitch
This popular stitch can be used to outline motifs. To work the stitches, take the needle through the fabric on the right side and bring it up again to the right side a short distance

Running stitch

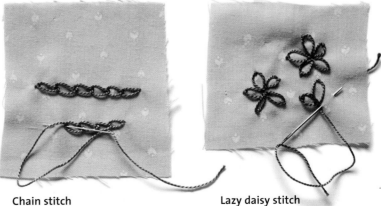

Chain stitch

Lazy daisy stitch

away, looping the yarn around the needle in small circle before making the stitch.

Lazy daisy

This is a variation on the chain stitch and, as the name implies, it makes a pretty daisylike design. Basically work a normal chain stitch, but then take a further small securing stitch at the tip of each chain. Work five stitches in a circle to make a little daisylike flower.

Cross stitch

A geometric stitch in the straight stitch family, this is one of the most popular embroidery stitches in part because if you work it on an open-weave fabric, you can create very neat little rows of stitches. I prefer a more freehand version, and find the irregularity adds to the charm. Work one part of the diagonal cross (from bottom right to top left) and then take the needle and thread behind the work to create the opposite-diagonal that crosses it. Continue along the line in this way.

Seed stitch

Seed stitch is so called because it looks like seeds scattered on the ground. It is made with a series of tiny stitches that can face in different directions, to produce a random effect. It can be used to fill areas with colour to create a light and sparkly effect.

French knots

These are raised stitches formed into little knots by winding the thread around the needle three or four times in the course of making the stitch, so that each stitch resembles a small bead. It can be hard to create evenly formed knots, so practise first on a piece of spare fabric if you want a professional-looking finish.

Cross stitch

Seed stitch

French knots

Machine stitching

You need to be able to use a sewing machine for many of the projects in this book. Sewing machines vary so it is important to refer to the manual for specific instructions.

You should always do a practice sample first when using new fabrics and threads to check the stitch tension is correct.

Two fairly simple stitches are required: straight stitch (a machine form of backstitch) and zigzag stitch, which as the name implies, forms a zigzag line of stitches.

Seams are stitched using straight stitch. To stitch them on medium weight cotton with standard cotton thread, set your machine to this facility and adjust the stitch length to around 2.5.

For decorative stitching or for neatening edges or seams, you can use zigzag stitch. Again, for standard weight cottons, set your machine to this facility and use 2.5 for a basic zigzag, or adjust the stitch length if you wish to make longer zigzags.

To stitch a seam
Place the fabric to be stitched right sides together. If the pieces are small, you don't need to pin them, but longer seams will need to be pinned first (at right angles to the stitching line). Straight stitch parallel to the edge, roughly 1cm (½in) from it, to allow for the fabric fraying. Neaten the frayed edges with zigzag stitch if you wish.

To make a simple bag shape
Place two rectangles of fabric cut to the size required right sides facing. Stitch around the edges, leaving a 1cm (½in) allowance all around. Turn the shape inside out and finish off the raw edge by folding the right side to the wrong side and stitch it in place.

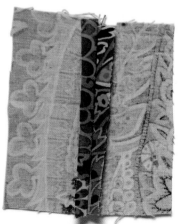

Straight seam

Making a bag

To gather fabric

For the bag on page 48 you will need to gather the fabric before you stitch it to the part that holds the handles.

1 Machine stitch along the raw edge using a fairly long stitch.

2 Then mark the required width with a pin and draw up the loose threads of the machine stitching to draw the fabric to the required size.

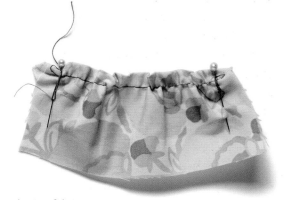

Gathering fabric

To make a Suffolk puff

These are used to decorate several projects in the book. You can make soft ones, or more formal ones in which a button is inserted into the centre.

1 Cut out a circle of fabric to approximately twice the finished size that will be required. Then run a row of gathering stitches (hand or machine) around the edge.

2 Place a button in the centre of the circle. Pull up the threads to draw the fabric into a puff.

Making a Suffolk puff

Free-motion embroidery

Free-motion embroidery is done using a sewing machine with a special attachment called a darning foot. It's a small circular foot which allows you to move the fabric in all directions whilst stitching. To work free-motion embroidery you need to raise the feed dogs on your machine – these normally clamp the fabric in place.

You can work different kinds of stitches using free-motion embroidery, but I have generally used basic stitches such as straight (**A**) or zigag (**B**) in this book. You can form circles or coils by moving the fabric in a circular motion.

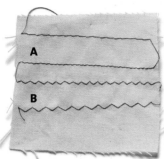

Basic stitches

Free-motion circles and coils

Free-motion outlines

Free-motion outlines onto a patterned fabric
Free-motion embroidery outlines are a quick way to embellish patterned fabric. You can add definition or highlight areas by simply machining around the shapes and patterns. Use a contrasting colour for the thread to get maximum definition.

Free-motion quilting
Free-motion embroidery can also be used to attach quilting together. Sandwich your wadding in between two layers of fabric and then work into the patterns or floral within the fabric. This is a lovely technique for adding interesting textures to the surface of the fabric.

Free-motion quilting

Appliqué

Appliqué is a great technique for exploring and combining pattern on pattern. It's a technique that I use a lot in my work; I find it great for adding florals, patterned and printed fabrics as an embellishment to denim or plain fabric. Fabrics can be appliquéd using fusible sprays and Bondaweb or by hand or machine stitches – I use them all in this book.

Bondaweb appliqué

Bondaweb is used to quickly and efficiently fuse two fabrics together. Cut out two similar sized squares, one from your chosen appliqué fabric and one from the Bondaweb. Place the Bondaweb, rough side down onto the back of the square of fabric and use an iron to melt the glue. The Bondaweb is now stuck to the fabric, at this stage you can cut our shapes or around florals. Peel the backing paper from fabric; place the appliqué shape onto your chosen plain fabric and iron again to fuse both fabrics together. For a different effect use pattern on pattern.

Machine stitch appliqué

Simply cut out shapes from patterned fabric and pin onto plain fabric. For circles or intricate shapes use the darning foot on your sewing machine and free-motion stitch around the shapes to secure them in place. To avoid fabric moving around use the Bondaweb technique before machine stitching.

Hand appliqué

Cut shapes from patterned, printed or floral fabric and pin onto ground fabric. Hand stitch around the shapes. To vary the design use different decorative stitches such as chain, running stitch or French knots (see pages 10-11) . Again, to prevent the appliqué fabric moving as you stitch, use Bondaweb.

Bondaweb appliqué

Machine stitch appliqué

Hand appliqué

Adding sparkle

You can do this in various ways by adding rhinestones, beads and sequins. The choice of decoration and the manner in which you apply it will depend on the effect you want – casual or smart.

Iron-on rhinestones

Iron–on rhinestones are a great invention! They are so quick and easy to use and produce stunning effects. They come in a range of designs but can often look more effective when cut into segments and re-placed onto fabric.

Simply peel off the backing paper and place the motif face down onto fabric. The motifs are slightly sticky so they will stay in place as you iron the backs. Turn fabric over and apply heat, using an iron, for a few minutes in order to melt the glue on the rhinestones.

Peel back the top plastic to reveal a stunning rhinestone embellishment.

Beads and sequins

Beads can be attached to decorate fabrics. I like to combine them with rhinestones and hand stitch for an interesting surface pattern. Beads or sequins can look fantastic in the centre of florals and can really lift and enhance pattern.

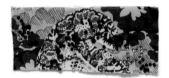

Stitch beads close together for intense decoration or just add one here and there for a more delicate effect.

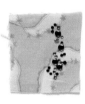

Or, for a more formal effect, use them to enhance a simple geometric pattern, such as stripes or checks.

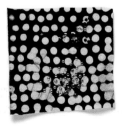

Ribbon rosette base

The ribbon rosette on page 61 is created from a concertina ribbon base as shown below. The size of rose depends on the length of ribbon.

1 When making a ribbon rosette, you need first to fold it at the centre to form a right angle.

2 Continue to make folds, one side over the other, until the length of ribbon is used up.

3 Hold the ends of the ribbon together and let the folded part fall away, Hold onto one end to start pulling the ribbon into the rose shape.

Crochet flower base

You can make a crochet flower base by working a foundation chain of around 8 stitches in your chosen yarn, and joining this into a circle (**A**). Then work 10 single crochet stitches into the circle at intervals to form the petals (**B**). Once you have completed all the petals, you can work over each of these in single crochet again, to form a thicker flower (**C**). The size will vary according to the yarn chosen and the number of stitches worked.

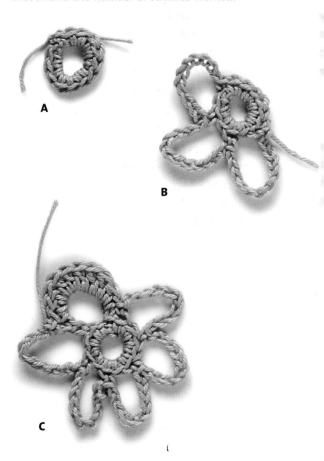

A

B

C

designs

to make

T-shirt

This T-shirt project is great for adults and children – both to make and to wear! It uses the simplicity and charm of a child's drawing as the basis for layers of decorative embellishment on top. Your choice of decoration will clearly be determined by the style and shape of your illustration, but for the one shown here I used ready-made heart and flower motifs embellished with appliqué and simple embroidery.

You can make all kinds of decorated surfaces using the basic principles outlined overleaf, not only for clothes but for canvas bags, pencil cases or bed linen, even making a grown-up version for yourself, perhaps using a photograph instead of a drawing as the basis for your design.

Before you begin

First you will need to transfer your chosen drawing onto heat transfer paper (see below). Once you have fixed the design to the T-shirt, you can decorate it as you wish by adding additional appliqué fabric, beads, buttons and embroidery stitches.

TO USE HEAT TRANSFER PAPER

Scan or photocopy your drawing onto the special heat transfer paper following the manufacturer's instructions. Cut out some of the shapes in the picture. Place all the pieces of heat transfer paper with the image face down onto the T-shirt. Move the different elements around until you are happy with the design. Using a hot iron, follow the manufacturer's instructions to iron and transfer the image from the paper pieces to the fabric. Peel off the backing paper.

To decorate the T-shirt

1 Use the heart and flower motifs to decorate and enhance the picture by placing them around the centre image. Add some extra cut out circles and a flower from floral fabric and pin onto the design.

2 Add printed fabric to the central image, and add additional appliqué leaves to the base, and pin to the T-shirt.

3 Use a hot iron to fix the iron-on red heart motifs to the T-shirt, following the manufacturer's instructions.

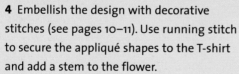

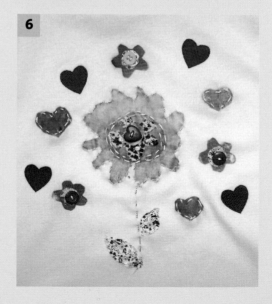

4 Embellish the design with decorative stitches (see pages 10–11). Use running stitch to secure the appliqué shapes to the T-shirt and add a stem to the flower.

5 Sew a button to the central flower using contrasting embroidery thread.

6 Finish with a few assorted buttons stitched to the centre of the flower shapes.

peg dolls

These cute little peg dolls can be made very quickly and children will enjoy either helping you or making their own. The project gives instructions for making Lulu, but you can easily make the variations, or indeed create your own unique designs.

Peg dolls make perfect gifts for little girls, while older children will gain as much pleasure from making them as playing with them. Fill a doll's house with a range of characters or simply display them in a cute row on a shelf to decorate a room. They also look great in a box frame against a background of pretty fabric. I used Rowan fabric scraps for my dolls, but you can use any leftover fabrics in your workbox.

PEG DOLL VARIATIONS

Here is a selection of dolls for you to copy. The project explains how
to make Lulu (below), but you can adapt the instructions to make any
of those shown by varying the colours, the sparkly embellishments,
the yarn colours for the hair and the embroidery, and the position
and style of hand stitching. Each doll assumes a slightly different
character, depending on the colours and fabrics chosen, so no two are
ever quite the same – look at Anna, Penny and Pat!

Made as they are on a peg base, which measures 12cm (5in) high,
these dolls are tiny, so you need to keep the design fairly simple in
order to be able to work it easily.

Lulu

Mishka

Penny

Poppy

Amelie

Anna

Eliza

Bianca

Juanita

Pippa

Cleo

Josette

Megan

Marie

Lizzie

Pat

MATERIALS

Rowan floral fabrics (in two toning colours)

Gold-Zack rhinestone transfer

Wooden clothes peg

Anchor Pearl Cotton, pink

Coats felt, pink

Anchor Pearl Cotton, deep pink and yellow

Coats button

Gold-Zack fine satin ribbon, pink

Felt marker pens or biros, red and black

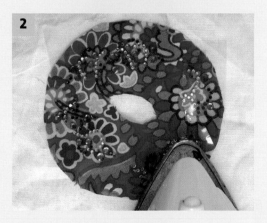

To make the skirt

1 Cut a circle out of the Rowan floral fabric measuring 10cm (4in) in diameter. Cut a smaller circle, 1.5cm (½in) in diameter out of the centre of the larger circle to leave you with a doughnut shape.

2 Decorate the skirt with the iron-on rhinestones following the manufacturer's instructions.

3 Push the wooden peg up through the small central hole in the skirt. Hand sew a line of running stitch (see page 10) around the 'waist' and pull the thread tight to secure the skirt shape to the peg.

To make the top

4 Cut a rectangle from the floral fabric measuring 6 x 2.5cm (2¼ x 1in). Fold over the top edge of the fabric to neaten and wrap the piece around the peg, securing with a pin.

5 Attach the fabric at the back to the peg with a little glue and then stitch the overlapping edges together to secure.

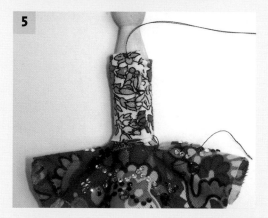

To make the wrap

6 Cut a semicircle shape from the piece of pink felt, measuring 14cm (5½in) in diameter.

7 Wrap the pink felt around the peg and stitch in place at the front using matching embroidery thread.

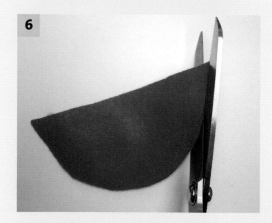

8

8 Using the pink thread, sew a button in a contrasting colour to the front of the wrap to cover the join.

To make the hair

9 Cut strands of yellow Pearl Cotton, 4cm (1½in) long, to make the hair.

10 Place a spot of PVA glue onto the round top, the 'head', of the peg.

11 Press the strands of thread onto the glue, smoothing them down to create a hairstyle.

9

11

10

To make the hat

12 Cut a circle from the fabric used for the skirt, approximately 4cm (1½in) in diameter, and a smaller circle of pink felt.

13 Stitch the circles together using running stitch around the smaller circle. Gather the thread to give a floppy hat shape.

14 Glue the hat onto the head of the doll to finish off the peg doll's outfit.

To make the face

15 Draw the face (as shown in photograph) using felt marker pens and/or a biro.

greeting card

This delightful card uses simple machine stitching to enhance the shape and patterns of a printed image. Photograph your favourite peg doll made in the project on pages 30–33, and machine or hand stitch embellishments to the design to give an extra dimension to a special hand-made greeting card. This is a great way of using up any leftover scraps of fabric or odd buttons and beads, and can be made to suit a range of occasions, from birthdays to a wedding or new baby cards, depending on the style of the peg doll.

You could use the basic concept in other ways, too. Simply print out an image (such as a portrait, perhaps, for an anniversary gift or a picture of your pet) and work over it in the same way. You'll be sure to make a stunning and individual card every time!

MATERIALS

Plain card 21 x 30cm (8¼ x 12in)

Print out of peg-doll image

Rowan floral fabric

Gold-Zack flower motifs, green and pink

Gold-Zack sequin flower motif

Sylko sewing thread, yellow

Gold-Zack fine ribbon, pink

Matching button

Decorative hand-made paper (10 x 15cm/4 x 6in)

Spraymount

Anchor Pearl Cotton, pink

Making a printed image

Take a digital photograph or make a photocopy to obtain a print out of the peg doll with the image size measuring approximately 10 x 15cm (4 x 6in).

To make the card

1 Gather together all the materials you used to make the peg doll.

2 Using the peg doll image as a guide, cut out a semicircle from a piece of floral fabric to cover the skirt of the doll. Pin the fabric onto the card on top of the skirt. Using the sewing machine (with a free-motion foot, see page 14) stitch the fabric onto the image. Use matching thread and follow shapes and lines within the hair to add to the effect. Continue to machine stitch around the shape of the doll, tracing along the arms and around any patterns on the fabric.

3 Glue flower motifs and ribbon bows onto the doll's wrap and hat to add some sparkle.

4 When the glue is dry, cut out the peg doll shape, carefully cutting around the outline and the fabric.

5 Fold the plain card in half and cut down further if desired. Place the piece of decorative paper on the front of the card and mount the peg doll in the centre with spraymount. Add a simple frame of running stitches following the line of the hand-made paper.

cake card

This greeting card, decorated with a row of enticing fabric cupcakes, is very simple to make but looks really stunning. The motifs are stitched onto the card using the free-motion foot on a sewing machine, but you can experiment with hand stitching too, to add extra detail.

This simple form of appliqué is very versatile and, depending on the number of motifs, you can adapt the technique to suit tall, narrow cards, as here, or try a landscape format, or even a square with just one motif in the centre.

Create a range of different cards using interesting fabrics from charity shops, craft fairs or car boot sales. Repeat prints are ideal – character fabrics of fairies, action figures, boats, or cats and dogs could all make fantastic cards!

MATERIALS

Plain white card and matching envelope
Gold-Zack fine silk ribbon, pink
Rowan Cupcake fabric
Glue
Sylko thread
Anchor Stranded Cotton, to match

Selecting motifs

Choose a fabric with clearly-defined motifs
that, when cut out, will appear complete.
A plain background will ensure neat edges.

To make the card

1 Cut a piece of plain white card to the
desired size; here the card measures
16 x 20cm (7 x 8in). Fold the card in half
to achieve a narrow, portrait format.

2 Place the ribbon along the inside fold of the
card, tying it in a bow on the front. I think the
bow looks good if it's positioned slightly
towards the top of the card rather than in the
centre. Glue the bow into place to stop it
moving around and loosening. Trim the ends.

3 Cut out three cupcakes from the Rowan
fabric. Position the cakes one above the other
on the card, at equal distances apart, centred
on the width. Pin in place.

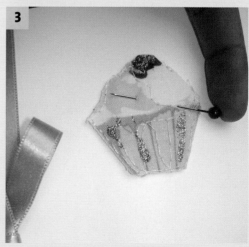

USEFUL TIPS

Use Bondaweb on your fabric shapes to attach them to the card before machine stitching. This will keep the shape in place and stop it from slipping whilst you are free machine stitching.

If you are using spraymount, use an old cardboard box as a shielded area into which to spray and always spray in a well-ventilated space.

To stitch on the motifs

4 Using the free-motion embroidery foot on the sewing machine, follow the outline of the cupcake shape to attach the fabric to the card. Repeat with the remaining cupcakes.

5 To add a little more decoration to the card, use the stranded cotton to add straight stitches and French knots (see pages 10–11), following the patterns printed on the fabric.

6 If you wish to cover the inside of the card, cut a piece of paper slightly smaller than your card and spraymount it to the inside.

denim jacket

Turn a wardrobe basic into a fun party piece by personalizing a classic denim jacket with your own choice of decoration. You can find denim jackets in charity and second-hand shops for very little expense, so there is no excuse not to have a go at creating your own version of this project.

The design shown here is quite fancy and uses lots of sparkly rhinestones together with appliqué flower motifs. You can make any variation on it you choose, but make sure you choose fabrics within a particular colour palette to give the design some cohesion.

If you prefer something simpler, perhaps for the pocket of a pair of jeans or along the hem, take a look at the designs on page 47.

MATERIALS

Gold-Zack rhinestone transfers

Coats felt, pink and green

Printed and velvet fabrics

Gold-Zack flower motifs

Vilene Bondaweb

Anchor Tapisserie yarn, to match

Anchor Stranded and Pearl Cottons, to match

3 Coats sparkly buttons

2

Planning the design

Decide on the area you wish to decorate and gather together the elements you will need, ensuring that their colours work together.

To add sparkle

1 To create the basis of the embellishment, cut the rhinestone transfers into small sections and place around the pocket area on the jacket. The rhinestones will add sparkle around the main flower motifs. Iron all sections of transfer into place (see page 16).

To make the leaf shapes

2 For the main body of the decoration you will need lots of different leaf shapes cut out from various fabrics. Cut one leaf shape from felt and use it as a template to cut leaves from a selection of fabrics, such as velvet, printed silk and felt. If desired, vary the sizes and shapes of the leaves.

3 Place all the fabric leaves onto a sheet of Bondaweb, pin in place and cut out the shapes. Use a hot iron to secure the fabric leaves onto the Bondaweb. Set aside.

To make the flower spray

4 Cut two small flower shapes from pink felt and cut small circular holes in the centre of each. Place each of the felt flowers over the centre of the iron-on flower motifs so that the beads come through the hole. Secure in place with a couple of hand stitches. Cut three lengths of green and orange tapestry yarn approximately 10cm (4in) long. Fold each strand in half and bundle the orange yarns together and the green yarns together. Pin a spray of felt leaves and one tapestry yarn bundle to each flower corsage and hand stitch together. The flower sprays are now ready to attach to the jacket.

To finish

5 Remove the backing paper from the remaining leaves and arrange leaves and flowers on the pocket area and attach with a hot iron. Arrange the decoration to flow across the spaces with the leaves spilling out.

6 Finish the jacket with three large sparkly buttons. Attach the buttons around the flower motifs with a simple hand stitch.

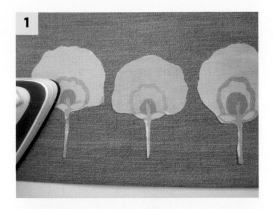

Hem decoration

Revive a pair of jeans or denim skirt with a little embellishment along the hem. Keep the design flat to avoid it catching as you move.

1 Cut out a motif from fabric. Attach to bondaweb and iron in place along the hem of jeans or a skirt.

2 Attach iron-on rhinestone transfers following the manufacturer's instructions, creating your own patterns.

3 With a contrasting thread, add some hand stitches to enhance the shape of the motif.

Pocket variation
Alternatively, add simple detail to a jacket or jeans pocket. Attach a gem or bead, and hand embroider a circular pattern around it (see pages 10–11). Contrasting threads and gems will add cohesion to the design.

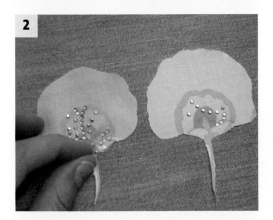

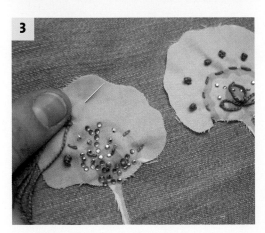

covered buttons

Breathe new life into your wardrobe by replacing old buttons with something new and exciting. Covered buttons are extremely decorative and very versatile – match them or contrast them to your garment for a touch of individuality. Each button will be different, with almost endless combinations of decorative details, from beads and sequins to delicate hand-embroidery stitches.

You don't have to use the buttons in the conventional way. They also look lovely attached to accessories, such as bags or gloves, and the large ones can even be pinned onto jackets and worn as cute little brooches.

MATERIALS

Prym cover button maker
Rowan printed fabric/Coats felt
Matching beads and sequins
Sylko threads, to match

Customizing covered buttons

There are myriad ways to customize covered buttons. You can embroider the fabric (see pages 10–11) or add stitch-on sequins and beads, then make the covered button in the usual way. To decorate an existing covered button, add small sections of iron-on transfer motifs.

To cover buttons

1 Select a metal cover button and cut a circle from your fabric to the size recommended by the button manufacturer.

1

2

3

2 Place the button in the centre of the fabric circle on the wrong side. Pull the fabric over the teeth, tucking it onto the prongs. Click the button back into place.

To make leaf and flower decorations
3 Cut out a simplified leaf and flower design from felt, or simple shapes of your own design, together with a circle of felt to cover the button, if you wish.

4

4 Stitch the leaf and flower shapes to the button fabric.

5 Apply a bead or sequin to the centre of the flower. Add some hand stitches if wished. Cover your button following steps 1–2.

5

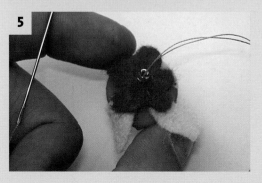

floral bag

This bag is simple to make and you can add whatever decoration takes your fancy. I chose to make some little crochet flowers and grouped these together at the top corner of the bag, but they would also look very effective in a row or placed diagonally from one corner down into the printed fabric. Play around with them before you make a decision and then attach them in place. If you are confident of your crochet skills, why not make three flowers in different sizes?

There are a couple of tips worth noting: when ruching fabric, it is best to draw up the gathering threads from either end. If you try and gather from one end only, you risk snapping your thread. Another useful tip is to cut both main pieces of the bag at the same time, so as to be sure that the curves match.

MATERIALS

Coats embossed felt fabric (for top of bag)

Rowan print fabrics (for bag and lining)

Sylko sewing thread

Set of Prym Viola handbag handles

Prym cover buttons

Anchor Pearl cotton

Patons 100% cotton yarn

Prym 3.5mm crochet hook

Prym clip-on rhinestones

Gold-Zack flower and sequin motifs

Gold-Zack rhinestone transfer

Anchor Stranded Cotton, to match

To make the bag

1 Cut out two pieces of felt fabric 30 x 10cm (12 x 10in). This will form the top of your bag. Cut two pieces of printed fabric 50 x 30cm (20 x 12in) for the lining. Fold over a 2.5cm (1in) hem on the lining fabric, press and pin in place.

2 Set your sewing machine to the loosest stitch length. Stitch along the hem on both pieces of lining fabric.

3 Pull one of the strands of thread at each end of the hem to ruffle up your fabric pieces to a width of 30cm (12in).

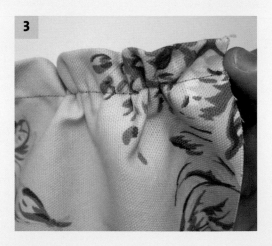

4 Lay both pieces of ruched fabric on top of each other, right sides together, and fold in half, with the ruffled hem at the top. Then cut a curved corner on the outer edge. When you open out the fabric you should have a symmetrical, curved base. Repeat steps 1–4 with the outer floral fabric and set aside.

To make the top

5 Fold over a 1cm (½in) hem on the top of both pieces of felt, pin and machine stitch.

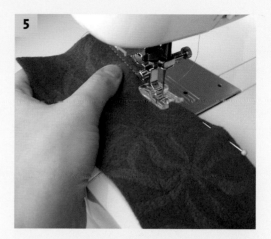

6 Pin both the outer floral bag pieces to the unhemmed raw edge of the felt, right sides together. (You will now have two pieces, one for the back and one for the front, with felt panels pinned in place.) Machine stitch each seam to create one piece from felt and printed fabric.

7 Pin both bag pieces together with right sides facing and machine along the seams, leaving the top felt edge open as this will be the opening for the bag. Trim the seams to neaten and turn inside out.

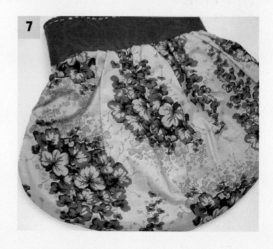

8 Now pin and stitch the lining together in the same way so that you are left with a separate bag from the lining material.

To add the floral decoration
9 Crochet three flowers (see page 17) in co-ordinating colours. Place sections of floral motifs in the centre of each flower or add a button or a group of pearls, beads or sequins and stitch in place.

To finish
10 Stitch the bag handles into place by hand on the inside hem of the felt.

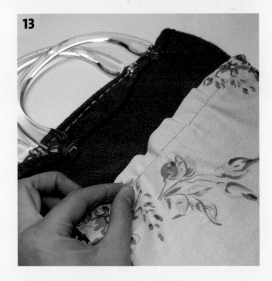

11 Add some covered buttons for extra decoration. Cover two metal cover buttons with co-ordinating fabric (see page 50) and stitch onto the outside of the bag at the base of the handle. Add French knots or beads to the buttons for that extra bit of sparkle.

12 Add a line of running stitch in a contrasting thread and some rhinestones to finish the embellishments.

13 Attach your lining. Simply place the lining bag into the main bag and hand stitch neatly to the felt top.

fascinator

This little hat is very easy to make and great for special occasions. You will need a raffia hat comb base to decorate with fabric and a selection of buttons, ribbons and rhinestones, plus of course the veiling which gives it its allure. The veiling is very versatile, allowing you to create some great shapes for the fascinator base. Before sewing the veiling to the base why not explore different shapes? You may like to have some of the veiling coming down over your face. Instead of buttons, you could add a group of pearls or beads to the veiling.

The fascinator bases can be bought ready-made in a range of different colours, as can the veiling. If your base doesn't already have a hair comb attached you will need to stitch one to it; this will allow you to keep it in place on your head.

Raffia hat comb base

Veiling

A selection of Coats buttons

Silk fabric

Small piece of patterned fabric

Large cover button

Prym clip-on rhinestones

Sylko sewing thread

Planning the design

This design is one you can adapt to suit your outfit. Place the decoration on the hat before stitching to see how the different colours and shapes work.

To make the base

1 Lay out the hat base and veiling and your button collection. You may also like to add beads and rhinestones.

2 Coil and arrange the veiling into a circular shape. Secure in place with a pin.

3 Once you have created your desired shape hold it against the fascinator base and stitch it securely in place through the buttons. The base of your head piece is now ready to decorate.

To make a silk rose

4 Fold in the raw edges of your silk fabric and fold the length in half, press and stitch down the length using the sewing machine. Follow the steps for making a ribbon rose base (see page 17). Holding one end of the ribbon, pull so that the central folded ribbon bunches to make the rose shape. Secure with a stitch in the centre.

5 Ruche and stitch the patterned fabric around the ribbon rose to give an outer flower effect. Place and stitch a button into the centre of the rose.

To finish

6 The flower can now be on stitched in place on the fascinator base. You can position the flower in the centre of a coil shape so that the veil sweeps around the flower. Stitch some small beads into the flower decoration and in between the gaps on the button base. Position the clip-on rhinestones randomly on the veiling to add some sparkle.

crochet brooches

You can make very pretty brooches using a combination of stitching and crochet techniques, with some ribbons, buttons and beads for embellishment. The following project gives instructions for a large, corsage style of brooch, together with an alternative, smaller version.

The central detail on both brooches is surrounded by crocheted petals. Even if you have never crocheted before, this technique is very easy to do and fun to learn. You can also customize it easily to suit your own requirements, making the petals more or less pronounced as you wish, or including a double layer of crochet petals.

MATERIALS

Rowan floral fabrics

Floral ribbon

Gold-Zack wide ribbon

Coats large sparkly button

Rowan Kidsilk Haze 4-ply yarn, pink

2.5mm crochet hook

Sylko thread, matching

Prym brooch pin

Coats felt

Choosing a colour scheme

When putting the different elements together, make sure that the colours of the fabrics and yarns, and the ribbon embellishment, harmonize together.

To make the large brooch

1 Cut a circle measuring 8cm (3in) n diameter from Rowan fabric and create a Suffolk puff (see page 13) to make the central part of the brooch.

2 Using either a floral ribbon or a strip of fabric, make a mini rosette in the centre of the Suffolk puff, by pleating and hand stitching to attach it to the centre.

3 Cut a length of ribbon and tie it around the shank of the sparkly button, so that the ends hang down like a rosette. Trim the ends of the ribbon neatly. Stitch the button to the centre of the brooch. Alternatively, you could use a cluster of beads, a covered button or sequins.

4 Make the lacy crochet trim for the edge of the Suffolk puff (see below). Pin in place around the edge and then stitch to secure with matching thread.

5 Finally, attach a pin back to the reverse of the brooch. For a neat finish, cover any stitching with a small circle cut from felt, before attaching the pin.

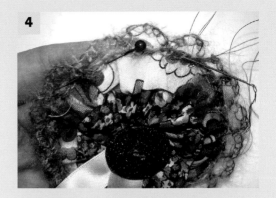

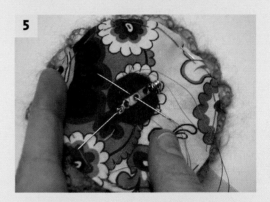

TO MAKE THE CROCHET EDGE

Crochet a chain long enough to go around the circumference of the Suffolk puff. You create the lacy effect by turning the work, working five chains and then working back into your original chain. For this design, I worked into every third stitch on my original chain but you can adjust the loops if you wish.

To make a small brooch

A good way to pull two different colours together is to use a patterned fabric. The final brooch measures 8cm (3in) in diameter.

1 Using blue yarn, crochet a large flower with lots of petals following the instructions on page 17. To do this, work your initial circle, chain 10 and join back into the circle in the next stitch. The flower should have 12 petals very close together.

2 Crochet a 6-petal red flower using cotton yarn. Place on top of the blue flower and hand stitch together.

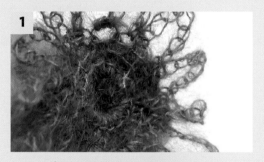

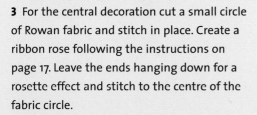

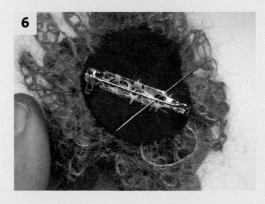

3 For the central decoration cut a small circle of Rowan fabric and stitch in place. Create a ribbon rose following the instructions on page 17. Leave the ends hanging down for a rosette effect and stitch to the centre of the fabric circle.

4 If liked, thread approximately 15 small beads onto a needle. Add a larger wooden bead to the end and attach the threaded beads just beneath the ribbon rose.

5 To finish, attach the fabric circle and embellishments to the crochet flowers.

6 Stitch a brooch back to the reverse.

bag charm

Transform a ready-made handbag charm by adding colourful pompoms.

These charms look great adorning bags, jeans or rucksacks. Use your

ingenuity to devise your own special pompoms. For an individual look

use strips of fabric, leather, yarn, ribbon and cotton. To customize the

charms even further, add decorative covered buttons (see pages 48-51),

large chunky beads and ribbon. Let your imagination run wild and use

wire to tie on small found objects, such as toys or keepsakes.

   When choosing a colour scheme, it is more effective to use a limited

palette, such as all hot colours (pinks, reds, oranges, yellows) or all cool

colours (blues, mauves, greens).

MATERIALS

Prym handbag charm
Prym pompom maker or card
Anchor Tapisserie wool (in chosen colours)
Narrow strips of Rowan printed fabric (in toning colours)
Gold-Zack fine ribbon
Prym cover buttons

Choose a style

This bag charm can have either two or three pompoms in two sizes, each using slightly different fabrics.

To make the pompoms

1 Use a pompom maker or cut out two cardboard doughnut shapes to the size required. Wrap yarn and strips of fabric around the pompom maker as shown, until the central hole is full.

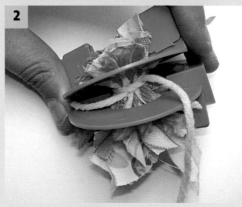

2 Snip around the entire edge of the circle, and then pull the pieces of cardboard apart to leave a small gap in the centre of the pompom. Tie a length of string or yarn around the centre to secure all the threads and strips together. Remove the card.

3 Tighten the string and fluff up the pompom. Trim any surplus ends to neaten the shape. Attach to the charm with ribbon.

4 Make up the next pompom following steps 1–3, but this time use slightly larger cardboard pompom shapes. When complete, tie onto the handbag charm.

5 If required, make up a third pompom to the same size as the second one, and tie onto the handbag charm.

corsage

A corsage adds a stylish finishing touch to any outfit. They look great worn on lapels but are also fun worn on sweaters, bags, hats and fascinators (see pages 58-61). Stunning customized corsages are easily put together using a shop-bought corsage base, which is then embellished with your own choice of decorations. The one shown here has a simple covered button (see pages 48-51) as the central part of the decoration. You can vary the style of the corsage while still following the basic instructions given here, simply by changing colourways or adding a little extra sparkle for evening wear. The steps overleaf show a similar, but more decorated, version of this one.

Preparation

You will need to replace some of the petals from the existing corsage. Cut out some of the petals from the corsage ready to replace with new fabric petals.

To make the petals

1 Using the petals you have cut from the corsage as a template, draw five new petals onto patterned fabric.

2 Following the templates, cut out all five of the new petal shapes.

3 Hand stitch the five petals back into the corsage to replace the old ones. The new petals will add extra colour and pattern to your corsage.

To decorate the corsage

4 Cut five lengths of co-ordinating ribbon, approximately 8cm (3in) long. Stitch each length of ribbon into the centre of the corsage. Position the ribbon over the petals, with all lengths an equal distance from each other. (Your stitching at the centre of the corsage will be hidden with a covered button.)

5 Decorate a covered button as desired, with rhinestone transfers, beads, sequins or simple hand stitches (see pages 10–11). Once the button is ready, place it in the centre of the corsage and stitch into place.

6 Finally, on the reverse side of the corsage, glue any loose ends in place.

gadget cover

This little drawstring bag is perfect to hold and protect either an MP3 player or a mobile phone. You could personalize it with motifs or by using different fabrics. It makes a great little project that can be adapted to suit teenagers or adults!

If you are going to keep your gadget cover in your handbag it will need to be fairly robust. You may like to try variations of embellishment but always keep in mind that it needs to be securely attached to the fabric in order to withstand a lot of wear-and-tear and handling.

Hardwearing fabrics

Corduroy is a good choice for this bag as it is soft to the touch but relatively strong. Felt or wool will also wear well and add some protection for the bag's contents.

To make the decoration

1 Cut two pieces of corduroy fabric approximately 10 x 15cm (4 x 6in) each.

2 Draw a simple flower outline on plain fabric and cut it out, or cut out a suitable flower motif from printed floral fabric. Pin the flower onto the right side of one piece of corduroy.

3 Free-machine embroider the centre of the flower to stitch it in place (see page 14). Zigzag stitch around the outside.

4 Using Anchor Pearl thread, embroider a few French knots and some straight stitches (see pages 10–11) and finally a couple of beads for some sparkle on the flower.

To make up the bag

5 Fold a 1cm (½in) hem on the top edge of each piece of corduroy. Cut a length of ribbon to make the drawstring, and enclose it in the folded hem. Cut a small hole on either side of the hem and pull the ribbon out of the holes (ready to be pulled tight, ruching the bag). Using the sewing machine, stitch the drawstring hems in place.

6 Place the two pieces of fabric right sides together and stitch a seam along three sides, leaving the top open. Trim the seam close to the line of stitching. Turn right sides out. Place your mobile phone or MP3 player inside and simply pull the ribbon drawstring tight to close up the little bag.

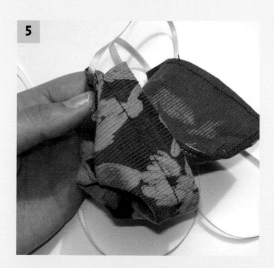

VARIATION

If you want to make a more girlie version of the bag, use a silky fabric or a crushed velvet for the cover, but line it in a thicker fabric to provide protection. This little bag in mauves and pinks is decorated with little fabric roses (see pages 16 and 61), along with sparkly rhinestones and beads.

This gorgeous little doggy coat is perfect for any pampered pooch princess. It's a great project to experiment with combined appliqué, embellishment and machine-quilting techniques.

If you are making the coat for a male dog, you can change the fabric colour and pattern. If you have male and female dogs the same size, you could always make the coat reversible and have it girly on one side and a bit more 'manly' on the other.

I've appliquéd florals onto the tweed but if you wanted to create a different effect you could use smaller shapes, prints or patterns – even an illustrated doggy fabric!

doggy coat

Preparation

This project is a little more challenging than others and will take a little longer. Allow plenty of time and double-check measurements to ensure that the coat fits your dog. I used a sewing machine to make the quilting, but you can do this by hand if you prefer, although it will take longer.

To cut out the pattern

1 Measure your dog to make sure that the coat will fit snugly. Take measurements around your dog's tummy and neck, and for the length of the back from the base of the head to the base of the tail. The coat will not reach all the way around your dog's middle as straps will be added, so allow two-thirds of this area for the width of the coat.

2 On a piece of tracing or pattern paper, draw out a rectangle corresponding to the measurements you have taken. Cut out your paper pattern piece. (You can try the paper pattern piece on your dog to check the measurements, making any adjustments for fit beforepinning it onto the tweed fabric).

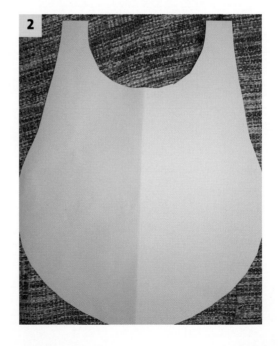

3 Cut out the tweed fabric. Fold in half along its length. Mark and cut a curve along one short edge, so that when the fabric is opened out you have a semicircular edge. Use the same method to cut out the neck shape. Use the tweed fabric as a template to cut out the lining fabric.

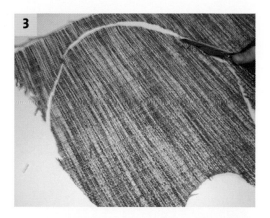

To embellish the coat

4 Cut a section of your chosen patterned fabric large enough to cut out appliqué shapes, here I've used a floral print. Cut out pieces of Bondaweb the same size as your fabric. Iron Bondaweb onto the back of the floral fabric. Cut shapes from the fabric following patterns within the print. Peel off the backing paper from the Bondaweb and pin the flowers randomly onto the tweed. Iron in place. The flowers are now ready for further decoration.

5 To give the coat some warmth and thickness, I have added a layer of wadding. Simply use the coat as a template to cut out a piece of wadding and pin it to the back of the tweed. Now machine stitch around the attached flowers with the free-motion foot and you will get an interesting machine quilted look. To add sparkle use metallic thread, such as Anchor Alcazar.

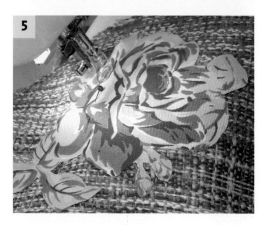

6 For extra decoration, add some hand stitching to the appliquéd shapes and apply small areas of rhinestone transfers (see page 16) on top of the flowers.

7 To further enhance the embellishment, add a few hand embroidered French knots (see page 11) in a co-ordinating thread.

To make the straps

8 Using the same patterned fabric as for the appliqué, cut a strip approximately 25 x 10cm (10 x 4in). Cut in half along its length, right sides together, and machine stitch a 1cm (½in) hem along the two long and the one short edge.

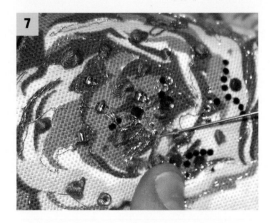

9 Trim the seam and turn the fabric inside out. Cut the strip in half so that you now have two pieces to use as straps. Fold in the raw edges of one end of each strap, pin and slip stitch closed. You are now ready to sew up the doggy coat.

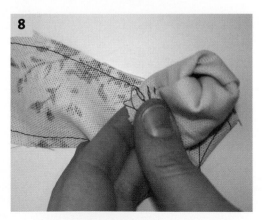

To finish

10 Place the outer tweed fabric and the lining fabric right sides together. Insert the open ends of the straps on either side of the coat and pin in place, ensuring they are exactly opposite each other.

11 Try the coat on your dog and see where the most comfortable place is for the tummy straps to be fastened. Machine stitch around the outer edge of the coat, leaving a small opening to turn out.

12 Trim the seams neatly and turn the coat inside out. Turn in the opening and slip stitch it closed.

13 Hand stitch a length of ribbon onto each side of the neck, long enough to fasten comfortably around the dog's bib. Finally, stitch strips of Velcro onto the tummy straps so you can secure the coat around the middle.

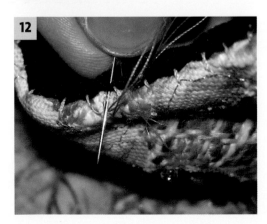

sparkly silk scarf

This project uses appliqué to add a splash of colour and pattern to a floral silk scarf. However, you can also use fabrics in a more innovative way by taking interesting sections of a patterned fabric to appliqué onto a plain scarf. By cutting a variety of shapes from fabric you can play around with scale and add pattern on pattern. Appliqué is also a great way to introduce and bring together a new colour scheme.

This project is a perfect opportunity to experiment with design and pattern. You can make your own scarf, as here, or look out for old scarves in charity shops, and use vintage fabrics or try cutting up old clothes for a more retro feel.

MATERIALS

Floral silk fabric (0.25m/¼yd)
Gold-Zack rhinestone transfer
Gold-Zack Flower sequin flower motifs
Sylko thread
Anchor Pearl Cotton
Anchor Stranded Cotton
Prym clip-on rhinestones

Planning your design

Make the centre of the embellishment very intense and try to create swirling fluid shapes.

To make the scarf

1 Cut two long strips of silk fabric, 1cm (½in) wider than the width and length you require to allow for turnings

2 To embellish the scarf, position the flower motifs around the bottom end of each strip. Pin and iron in place as required. To add sparkle, cut the motif into various segments and apply onto the scarf around the central design. Use an iron to fix sparkly rhinestones to the fabric (see opposite).

3 For extra decoration, add lazy daisy and French knots (see pages 10–11) around the floral motifs. A simple running stitch, following patterns within the fabric, looks very effective.

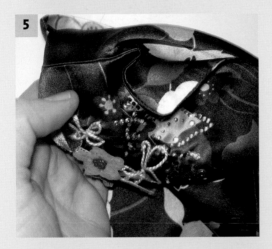

USEFUL TIP

Ironing the rhinestones in place from behind is the best and quickest way to melt the glue and make sure everything is securely fused in place. Place the rhinestones on the right side of the fabric.

4 Pin both lengths of silk together with right sides facing. Machine stitch both lengths and across one end, leaving the other end open for turning.

5 Trim the seams to neaten and turn the scarf right sides out. Press the scarf with an iron. Fold in the open end, press and pin in place.

6 Close the open end with a simple slip stitch.

vintage gloves

Decorating vintage kid gloves creates a very elegant and special accessory. Try to make the pattern of the decoration flow across the glove, so that there aren't any harsh edges. Add beads in clusters in the centre of florals or use sequins alongside French knots for extra surface texture.

This project employs a number of skills, including hand embroidery and appliqué. Silk is a lovely fabric to use here as these gloves are old and very delicate, but you could always vary the design and use a bright-coloured, retro pair of gloves with elements of a bold 70s print for a more funky look!

MATERIALS

One pair soft leather gloves

Patterned silk fabric

Vilene Bondaweb

Gold-zack rhinestone transfers

Prym clip-on rhinestones

Decorative crochet flowers

Vintage crochet trim

Leather needle

Anchor Pearl Cotton, to match

Gold-Zack narrow ribbon

4 Prym cover buttons

Planning your design

Build the design in stages, adding the final touches once the base design is complete. Add decoration around the cuff where you can work a needle through the glove.

To make the fabric appliqué

1 Cut enough small shapes from the patterned silk fabric to cover the top of each glove. Iron bondaweb onto the back of each of the silk fabric shapes, peel off the backing paper and pin the shapes in place. I've arranged them in a cluster, moving from the top edge of the gloves down towards the fingers. Carefully iron on all the fabric shapes, using the tip of the iron to fuse the Bondaweb and taking care not to iron onto the leather.

To embellish the gloves

2 Start to build up the layers of embellishment with the rhinestone motifs. Cut the motifs into smaller sections and place on top of the fabric shapes (see page 16).

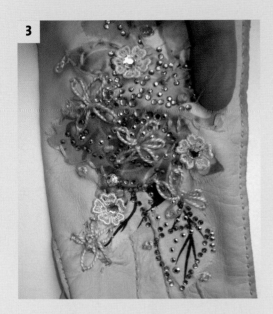

3 You are now ready to work into the design with hand stitches. Use simple stitches, such as lazy daisies in the centre of the embellishment and some small French knots scattered around them. Add crochet flower motifs, clip-on rhinestones, sequins or beads scattered across the gloves. The main body of the embellishment is now complete.

4 Hand stitch the vintage crochet trim around the top edge of the gloves using a leather needle. Make sure the trim protrudes over the edge of the gloves. Hand stitch matching ribbon onto the top of the gloves just underneath the crochet trimming. Add a row of French knots along the ribbon.

5 Tie the ends of the ribbon in a delicate bow and stitch down.

6 Cover four cover buttons with silk fabric and attach two to each glove, one in the centre of the ribbon bow and the other directly beneath.

Stockists and suppliers

The haberdashery, felt, decorations and most of the yarns used in this book are supplied by Coats Crafts UK. Many fabrics and some yarns are supplied by Rowan Yarns (a subsidiary of Coats Crafts UK). Their main addresses are listed below.

More detailed lists of stockists and suppliers can be found on their websites.

Detailed materials lists for the projects (with order numbers where appropriate) are shown here and on the following pages.

Coats Crafts UK
Lingfield Point
McMullen Road
Darlington, Co. Durham
DL1 1YQ
www.coatscrafts.co.uk
tel +44 (0)1325 394237

Rowan Yarns
Green Lane Mill
Holmfirth
HD9 2DX
www.knitrowan.com
tel +44 (0)1484 681881

T-shirt (page 20)
T-shirt
Child's picture
T-shirt heat transfer paper
Gold-Zack heart motifs 925, 220
Selection of Coats buttons 04193/e, 03815/d
Anchor Pearl Cotton, to match 359

Peg doll (page 26)
Rowan floral fabrics (in two toning colours)
Gold-Zack rhinestone transfer 926248
Wooden clothes peg
Anchor Pearl Cotton, pink 24
Coats felt, pink
Anchor Pearl Cotton, deep pink and yellow 69, 359
Coats button 507502
Gold-Zack fine satin ribbon, pink 982280
Felt marker pens or biros, red and black

Greetings card (page 34)
Plain card 21 x 30cm (8¼ x 12in)
Print out of peg-doll image
Gold-Zack flower motifs, green and pink 926132, 926133
Gold-Zack sequin flower motif 926158
Coats sewing thread
Gold-Zack fine ribbon, pink 982280
Matching button
Decorative hand-made paper (10 x 15cm/4 x 6in)
Spraymount
Anchor Pearl Cotton, pink 69

Cake card (page 38)
Plain white card and matching envelope
Gold-Zack fine ribbon, pink 982280
Rowan Cupcake fabric
Glue
Coats sewing thread
Anchor Stranded Cotton, to match 54

Denim jacket (page 42)
Gold-Zack rhinestone transfers 926249
Coats felt, pink and green
Printed and velvet fabrics
Gold-Zack flower motifs 926233
Vilene Bondaweb 902
Anchor Tapisserie yarn, to match 8164, 9096
Anchor Stranded and Pearl Cottons, to match 323, 206
3 Coats sparkly buttons 511551

Covered buttons (page 48)
Prym cover button maker 323153
Rowan printed fabric/Coats felt
Matching beads and sequins
Coats sewing thread

Floral bag (page 52)
Coats embossed felt fabric (for top of bag)
Rowan print fabrics (for bag and lining)
Coats sewing thread
Set of Prym Viola handbag handles
Prym cover buttons 323154
Anchor Pearl Cotton 97
Patons 100% cotton yarn green 1703, lilac 3333
Prym 3.5mm crochet hook 195138
Prym clip-on rhinestones 403365
Gold-Zack flower and sequin motifs 926158, 926160
Gold-Zack rhinestone transfer 926254
Anchor Stranded Cotton, matching 206

Fascinator (page 58)
Raffia hat comb base
Veiling
A selection of Coats buttons: 03743/c, 2930/3, 14625/3, 11525/3, 48235/3, 04053/e, 03283/f
Silk fabric
Small piece of patterned fabric
Large cover button 323164
Prym clip-on rhinestones 403365
Coats sewing thread

Crochet brooches (page 62)
LARGE BROOCH
Rowan floral fabrics
Floral ribbon
Gold-Zack wide ribbon shade 40
Coats large sparkly button 0479e
Rowan Kidsilk Haze 4-ply yarn, blue
2.5mm crochet hook 195136
Coats sewing thread
Prym brooch pin 081405
Coats felt
SMALL BROOCH
Patons 100% Cotton, red
Kidsilk Haze 4-ply yarn, blue
Prym 2.5mm crochet hook 195136
Rowan floral fabric
Gold-Zack fine silk ribbon, red 982275
Assorted beads
Prym brooch pin 081405
Coats sewing thread

Bag charm (page 68)
Prym handbag charm 417100
Prym pompom maker or card
Anchor Tapisserie wool (in chosen colours) 8416, 8038
Narrow strips of Rowan printed fabric (in toning colours)
Gold-Zack fine ribbon 982231
Prym cover buttons 323164

Corsage (page 72)
Prym corsage base 416750
Floral fabric
Gold-Zack narrow ribbon 982210
Prym large cover button 323164
Anchor Pearl Cotton (to match) 359
Gold-Zack sequin motif 926249
Decoration for button
Glue

Gadget cover (page 76)
Corduroy fabric
Floral fabric
Coats sewing thread
Anchor Pearl Cotton (to match) 69,326
Gold-Zack matching ribbon 982231
Jaeger beads, J3001007

Doggy coat (page 80)
Tracing or pattern paper
Tweed fabric
Corduroy lining fabric
Floral fabric
Vilene Bondaweb 902
Wadding
Anchor Alcazar Machine embroidery thread (to match) 9315/9317
Gold-Zack rhinstone transfers 926249
Anchor Pearl Cotton (to match) 24,69
Gold-Zack wide ribbon shade 40
Velcro

Sparkly silk scarf (page 86)
Floral silk fabric (0.25m/¼yd)
Gold-Zack rhinestone transfers 926249, 926260
Gold-Zack Flower sequin flower motifs 926158
Coats sewing thread
Anchor Pearl Cotton (to match)
Anchor Stranded Cotton (to match)
Prym clip-on rhinestones 403365

Gloves (page 90)
One pair soft leather gloves
Patterned silk fabric
Vilene Bondaweb 902
Gold-zack rhinestone transfers 926257
Prym clip-on rhinestones 403365
Decorative crochet flowers
Vintage crochet trim
Leather needle 131259
Anchor Pearl Cotton (to match)
Gold-Zack ribbon 982352
4 Prym cover buttons 323152

Acknowledgments

I would like to thank Susan, John and Anne for making the production of my first book a smooth and pleasurable one. Thanks to Danny, my parents, family and friends for their endless support and interest in my work. A special thank you for motivating me goes to my mum for pre-ordering five copies of the book months before I had even finished writing it. It worked ! You spurred me on to get it done! To my brother, Andy, who has always been the technical one, big thanks for helping me out with the graphics!

Charlotte Liddle

The publishers would like to thank Tara Heseltine and Maddy Daykin for modelling, as well as Ruth Smart and her dog, Monty.